I0841688

FROM RAGS TO RICHES

A Practical Guide to Building Wealth

WESLEY L. DIENER

Copyright © 2020 by Wesley L. Diener

Protected by copyright law.

No piece of this book might be utilized or replicated using any and all means, realistic, electronic, or mechanical, including copying, recording, taping, or by any data stockpiling recovery framework without the composed consent of the distributer with the exception of brief citations exemplified in basic articles and audits.

Table of Contents

CHAPTER 1

Introduction

1.1 The Journey Begins

Welcome to a life-changing adventure as we embark on the path from rags to riches. This book is your guide to transforming your financial situation and building lasting wealth. Get ready to explore the strategies, mindset shifts, and practical steps necessary to achieve your financial goals.

1.2 Defining Wealth

Wealth extends far beyond mere material possessions and monetary abundance. In this book, we will explore a comprehensive definition of wealth that encompasses financial freedom, personal fulfillment, and a sense of purpose. Discover how true wealth involves holistic well-being, including physical health, emotional balance, and meaningful connections with others.

Wealth is the total of assets (things you own) that give you financial security. The word wealth carries the idea of plenty and security.

If we were talking about a defined period in history, or any defined part of the world, then the definition of wealth would change depending on what was happening at the time and where it happened in the world. Today, most people use money, real estate, cars, stocks about which we chatter—to name a few aspects of wealth we hold. But if your parents had decided to have children a couple hundred years ago when the economy centered around agriculture, your parent's would have probably measured their children's wealth in terms of the commodities you own—coal, sugar, livestock and so on.

1.3 Why Building Wealth Matters

Understanding the importance of building wealth is essential for your journey. This book will present graphically the reasons why pursuing financial success is crucial for your overall well-being and the impact it can have on your life. Explore the freedom and opportunities that wealth provides, empowering you to create the life you desire and support your loved ones.

1.4 Overcoming Limiting Beliefs

Our beliefs about money and success often shape our financial reality. Learn practical strategies to challenge and overcome these obstacles, empowering you to develop a prosperous mindset and embrace a mindset of abundance.

Limiting beliefs about money are subconscious, but much of what you experience in your world is the result of these limiting beliefs that you don't check. These limiting beliefs can destroy your financial well-being and make you lose sight of what it's all about – growing wealth for yourself, family and friends.

The single most common limiting belief when it comes to making money is that if you work at a desk, then you have no hope of becoming rich. This is due, in part, to how you look at the world and what it has to offer. If you have this limiting belief (and many others), you may be blocking yourself from getting started on your path to riches.Whether they're conscious or not, lim riming about money will hold you in place.

As you embark on this transformative journey, be prepared to challenge your preconceived notions about wealth and discover new perspectives on what it truly means to be rich. Building wealth goes beyond amassing money; it involves aligning your values, pursuing personal growth, and creating a positive impact in your own life and the lives of others. Get ready to break free from limiting beliefs and set the stage for a remarkable financial transformation. The journey from rags to riches begins now.

CHAPTER 2

Laying the Foundation: Financial Mindset and Habits

2.1 Shifting Your Money Mindset

Your mindset plays a pivotal role in shaping your financial reality. The way you think about money, your beliefs, and your attitudes towards wealth can significantly impact your financial decisions and actions. If you aspire to build wealth and attain financial freedom, it is crucial to start by examining and shifting your money mindset.

Your views and beliefs about money are reflected in your money mindset. A positive money mindset can assist with directing your ways of behaving in a surprisingly strong manner, while a negative cash mentality can create similarly adverse outcomes.

Cash attitude is to a great extent impacted by previous encounters around cash. It's possible that your parents or grandparents taught you financial etiquette, but it's also possible that money was a taboo subject in your family. From that point, you've either deliberately or subliminally fostered a special arrangement of convictions toward cash in view of your background.

The first step in shifting your money mindset is becoming aware of your current beliefs and attitudes towards money. Identify any negative or limiting beliefs that may be holding you back from achieving financial success. Common limiting beliefs include thinking that money is scarce, believing that you are not capable of earning a significant income, or feeling guilty about desiring wealth. By acknowledging these beliefs, you can challenge and replace them with empowering thoughts and beliefs that align with your financial goals.

Next, immerse yourself in positive and abundant thinking about money. Surround yourself with resources that inspire and uplift your mindset, such as books, podcasts, or communities of like-minded individuals. Practice affirmations and visualization techniques to rewire your subconscious mind and reinforce positive money beliefs. As you consistently reinforce a mindset of abundance and opportunity, you will find yourself making better financial decisions and attracting wealth into your life.

2.2 Cultivating Wealth-Building Habits

Building wealth is not a one-time event but a result of consistent habits and behaviors that support your financial goals. Cultivating wealth-building habits is essential for long-term financial success. Start by creating a budget that aligns with your financial aspirations and helps you track your income and expenses. A budget provides a clear overview of your financial situation, allows you to allocate funds strategically, and helps you make informed decisions about saving, investing, and spending.

In addition to budgeting, saving regularly is a fundamental wealth-building habit. Set aside a portion of your income for savings, and make it a non-negotiable commitment. Automating your savings can make it easier to stay consistent. Consider setting up automatic transfers to a separate savings account or using apps that round up your purchases and save the difference. By making saving a priority, you create a financial cushion and accumulate funds that can be invested for future growth.

Another crucial habit to cultivate is prudent spending and wise financial decision-making. Before making a purchase, ask yourself if it aligns with your long-term financial goals. Practice delayed gratification by avoiding impulse buying and weighing the value of a purchase against its long-term impact on your financial well-being. By cultivating mindful spending habits, you can control your expenses, maximize your savings, and allocate more resources towards wealth-building endeavors.

Frugality is never a concept to be mistaken for those who don't have abundant cash relatively, but it should be well-learnt that frugality is a term for responsible utilisation of available financial resources within one's reach. Every individual who wishes to rise beyond ordinary financial level must be frugal in finance.

2.3 Managing Debt and Credit

Debt and credit can either be tools for wealth creation or burdens that hinder your financial progress. Managing debt and credit wisely is essential for building a solid financial foundation. Begin by assessing your current debt situation. Make a list of all outstanding debts, including credit card balances, loans, and mortgages. Understand the interest rates, payment terms, and repayment schedules for each debt.

To effectively manage debt, prioritize paying off high-interest debts first. Allocate extra funds towards these debts while maintaining minimum payments on others. Consider debt consolidation strategies, such as transferring balances to lower-interest credit cards or consolidating multiple loans into a single payment. Negotiate with creditors to explore options for lower interest rates or extended repayment terms.

Simultaneously, develop responsible credit

habits. Pay your bills on time to maintain a good credit history. Regularly review your credit report to identify any errors or discrepancies that may affect your creditworthiness. Use credit cards wisely by keeping balances low and paying them off in full each month. By managing debt and credit responsibly, you can reduce financial stress, improve your credit score, and position yourself for future wealth-building opportunities.

Remember, shifting your money mindset, cultivating wealth-building habits, and managing debt and credit are crucial steps in laying a solid foundation for building wealth. By adopting a positive money mindset, practicing smart financial habits, and effectively managing your debt and credit, you set yourself on a path towards financial prosperity and abundance. Embrace the power of mindset and habits as you embark on your journey from rags to riches.

2.4 Investing in Personal Growth

Investing in yourself is a key component of building wealth and achieving financial success. Personal growth and continuous learning contribute to your overall development, expand your capabilities, and increase your opportunities for wealth creation. By dedicating time and resources to invest in yourself, you lay a strong foundation for long-term financial growth.

One powerful way to invest in personal growth is by acquiring new skills and knowledge. Identify areas of expertise or fields that align with your interests and have potential for financial gain. Take courses, attend workshops, or pursue certifications to develop these skills. Whether it's improving your financial literacy, mastering a technical skill, or enhancing your communication abilities, ongoing learning equips you with valuable tools to thrive in various aspects of your life.

Beyond formal education, reading books, listening to podcasts, and consuming educational content can provide tremendous value for personal growth. Seek out resources that inspire and challenge your thinking, such as biographies of successful individuals, self-help books, or motivational podcasts. These resources can offer insights, strategies, and perspectives that expand your mindset and help you overcome obstacles on your wealth-building journey.

Investing in personal growth also involves seeking out mentors and coaches who can provide guidance and support. A mentor can offer valuable advice based on their own experiences and help you navigate challenges more effectively. A coach can provide accountability, help you set clear goals, and assist in developing action plans to achieve them. By leveraging the wisdom and expertise of others, you accelerate your personal growth and increase your chances of financial success.

Remember, personal growth is an ongoing process. Continually invest in yourself, seek opportunities for learning and development, and surround yourself with a network of like-minded individuals who inspire and support your growth. By investing in your personal growth, you enhance your abilities, increase your earning potential, and cultivate the mindset necessary for long-term wealth accumulation.

CHAPTER 3

<u>Building a Solid Financial Plan</u>

Financial planning provides a comprehensive overview of your current financial situation, future aspirations, and the strategies you've devised to achieve your goals. This essential process encompasses various aspects of your financial life, including cash flow, savings, debt management, investments, and insurance. By taking a holistic approach, financial planning ensures that all elements are carefully considered and integrated into a cohesive plan.

It's crucial to recognize that financial planning is an ongoing journey, continually adapting to your evolving circumstances and objectives. By examining your entire financial landscape, you can develop strategies that cater to both short-term and long-term goals, providing a roadmap for your financial success. A well-crafted financial plan not only alleviates money-related stress but also supports your current needs while laying the groundwork for future ambitions, such as a comfortable retirement.

The significance of creating a financial plan lies in optimizing your assets and gaining the confidence to navigate any financial challenges that may arise. Whether you choose to craft a financial plan yourself or seek guidance from a professional financial planner, the process is essential for maximizing your financial potential. With the advent of technology, online platforms like robo-advisors have made financial planning more affordable and accessible, allowing individuals to secure expert assistance in shaping their financial futures.

3.1 Setting Clear Financial Goals

Setting clear financial goals is the foundation of any successful wealth-building journey. When you have well-defined objectives, you have a clear vision of what you want to achieve and can align your actions and decisions accordingly. The first step in setting financial goals is to reflect on your aspirations and identify what truly matters to you. By establishing specific, measurable, attainable, relevant, and time-bound (SMART) goals, you create a roadmap that guides your financial decisions and actions. Once you have clarity on your goals, make them measurable by attaching numbers and timelines to them. For example, instead of aiming to "save money," set a specific target like "save $10,000 in the next 12 months."

To ensure your financial goals are attainable, it's important to assess your current financial situation. By evaluating your income, expenses, and any existing debts, you can determine how much you can realistically allocate toward your goals. Relevance is another key aspect of goal setting. Your goals should align with your values, priorities, and long-term vision for your life. By setting goals that are in line with your values, you'll have a stronger motivation to work towards them. Lastly, time-bound goals provide a sense of urgency and structure. Setting deadlines for your goals helps create a sense of accountability and allows you to track your progress along the way.

3.2 Budgeting: Your Pathway to Wealth

Budgeting is a fundamental tool for managing your finances effectively and building wealth. It is the process of creating a plan for your income and expenses, enabling you to track where your money is coming from and where it is going. By adhering to a budget, you can make informed decisions about your spending, saving, and investing. To create an effective budget, start by gathering information about your income sources, including your salary, side hustles, or investment returns. Then, list all your expenses, including fixed costs like rent/mortgage payments and utilities, as well as variable expenses like groceries, entertainment, and transportation.

Once you have a clear picture of your income

and expenses, it's time to evaluate your spending habits. By analyzing your discretionary spending, you can identify areas where you can cut back and save more money. For example, you could reduce dining out expenses by cooking more meals at home or find cost-effective alternatives for your entertainment needs. Additionally, it's important to prioritize your savings and investments in your budget. Allocate a portion of your income towards building an emergency fund, contributing to retirement accounts, and other wealth-building opportunities.

Regularly tracking and reviewing your budget is crucial for its success. Monitoring your expenses throughout the month ensures that you're staying on track. Consider using budgeting apps or spreadsheets to simplify the process and gain better visibility into your financial habits. As you continue to stick to your budget, you'll develop discipline, become more mindful of your spending decisions, and find opportunities to optimize your finances. Budgeting is not about restriction but rather about aligning your spending with your values and goals, ultimately leading you on the pathway to wealth.

3.3 Creating an Emergency Fund

Life is full of unexpected events, and having a

robust emergency fund is essential for financial stability and peace of mind. An emergency fund acts as a safety net, providing you with the means to navigate unexpected financial challenges without derailing your progress towards wealth. When building your emergency fund, it's important to set a regular savings goal. Determine how much you can contribute each month and make it a priority. Treat your emergency fund as a non-negotiable expense, just like paying your bills.

Automating your savings by setting up automatic transfers from your checking account to a separate savings account designated for emergencies ensures that you're consistently building your fund without having to rely on willpower alone. Keep your emergency fund separate from your daily spending accounts to avoid the temptation of dipping into it for non-emergency purposes. Choosing the right place to store your emergency fund is also crucial. While you want it to be easily accessible when needed, you also want it to earn some level of interest.

Look for high-yield savings accounts or money market accounts that offer competitive interest rates while providing liquidity. Avoid investments that carry a higher level of risk or have potential penalties for early withdrawal. Regularly reviewing and reassessing your emergency fund ensures that it remains aligned with your current financial situation and needs. With a well-funded emergency fund, you'll have the confidence and peace of mind to handle unexpected expenses or income disruptions without compromising your long-term financial goals.

CHAPTER 4

Maximizing Income: Career and Entrepreneurship

4.1 Identifying Your Skills and Passions

Identifying your skills and passions is a fundamental step in maximizing your income and achieving financial success. Your skills represent your unique talents, expertise, and strengths that set you apart from others. Recognizing and leveraging these skills can open doors to opportunities for career advancement and higher earning potential. By identifying your passions, you can align your work with what truly inspires and motivates you, leading to greater job satisfaction and a higher likelihood of success.

Understanding your skills requires self-reflection and evaluation. Take stock of your abilities, knowledge, and experiences. Consider what tasks come naturally to you and what you enjoy doing the most. These could be technical skills, such as coding or design, or soft skills like leadership or communication. Additionally, explore your passions and interests by reflecting on the activities that energize and excite you. What subjects do you find yourself constantly learning about or pursuing in your free time? By combining your skills and passions, you can identify career paths that offer both financial rewards and personal fulfillment.

Once you have identified your skills and passions, it's important to explore how they align with different industries and professions. Research potential career options that allow you to utilize and further develop your skills while engaging with topics that ignite your passion. Consider the market demand and growth potential in these fields to ensure long-term viability. Additionally, seek out opportunities for internships, part-time work, or projects that allow you to gain practical experience and validate your interests. The key is to find a balance between what you are good at and what you enjoy, creating a foundation for a fulfilling and lucrative career.

Furthermore, it's crucial to regularly reassess and update your skills and passions as you grow personally and professionally. Industries evolve, and new technologies emerge, so staying relevant and adaptable is essential. Continuously invest in your skills through professional development courses, certifications, or advanced degrees. Embrace a growth mindset and be open to learning and acquiring new knowledge. By continually refining and expanding your skills and aligning them with your passions, you can position yourself for ongoing success and income growth throughout your career journey.

4.2 Strategies for Career Advancement

To maximize your income and advance in your career, you need a strategic approach. Simply working hard may not be enough. It's essential to invest in your professional development to stand out and progress. Continuously upgrading your skills through further education, certifications, or workshops keeps you relevant in a rapidly evolving job market. Seek opportunities to enhance your knowledge and expertise, and stay informed about industry trends and advancements.

Networking plays a critical role in career advancement. Building relationships with mentors, colleagues, and industry professionals can lead to valuable connections and opportunities for growth. Attend industry events, join professional organizations, and actively engage with others in your field. Collaborating on projects or seeking guidance from experienced professionals can provide valuable insights and open doors to new career prospects.

Embracing a growth mindset is another essential strategy for career advancement. Be proactive in seeking additional responsibilities and challenges in your current role. Look for ways to contribute beyond your job description and demonstrate your leadership potential. Stay adaptable and embrace change, as industries evolve, and new technologies emerge. By positioning yourself as a lifelong learner and a valuable asset to your organization, you increase your chances of promotion and salary growth.

Furthermore, it's crucial to advocate for yourself and actively pursue opportunities for career advancement. This may involve seeking promotions, negotiating salary increases, or exploring new roles within your organization or industry. Keep track of your accomplishments and communicate your value to your superiors. Take the initiative to have conversations about your career goals and aspirations with your managers or mentors. By actively managing your career path and seizing opportunities for growth, you can accelerate your income potential and achieve long-term financial success.

4.3 Exploring Entrepreneurship

Entrepreneurship offers a unique pathway to maximize income and achieve financial freedom. As an entrepreneur, you have the opportunity to create and manage your own business ventures, paving the way for substantial financial rewards. However, it's important to approach entrepreneurship with careful consideration and planning.

Start by identifying a gap or unmet need in the market. Conduct thorough market research to understand your target audience, competitors, and potential demand for your product or service. Develop a solid business plan that outlines your value proposition, marketing strategies, and financial projections.

Risk is inherent in entrepreneurship, and not all ventures may succeed. It's crucial to embrace a resilient mindset and be prepared for challenges and setbacks along the way. Failure can be a valuable learning experience, providing insights for future endeavors. Seek support from mentors, join entrepreneurial communities, and build a network of like-minded individuals who can offer guidance and advice.

Furthermore, as an entrepreneur, you must be willing to take calculated risks and make decisions in uncertain environments. This requires a combination of strategic thinking, creativity, and adaptability. Stay focused on your long-term vision while being open to pivoting and adjusting your strategies based on market feedback and changing circumstances. Building a successful business takes time, effort, and perseverance, but with the right mindset and approach, entrepreneurship can offer substantial financial rewards and the flexibility to pursue your passions and dreams.

4.4 Building Multiple Streams of Income

Building multiple streams of income is a vital strategy for personal finance and wealth management. Relying solely on a single income source leaves you vulnerable to economic downturns, job loss, or unexpected financial emergencies. By diversifying your income streams, you spread your risk and increase your financial stability.

One way to build multiple income streams is through investments. Explore different investment options, such as stocks, bonds, real estate, or mutual funds. Investing in income-generating assets can provide passive income and potential capital appreciation over time. However, it's important to conduct thorough research and seek professional advice to make informed investment decisions that align with your risk tolerance and financial goals.

Additionally, consider exploring entrepreneurship as a means to create an additional income stream. Start a side business or pursue freelancing opportunities in your area of expertise. This allows you to leverage your skills and passions while generating supplemental income. While it may require extra time and effort, a successful side business can grow into a full-fledged entrepreneurial venture and provide a significant boost to your overall income.

Moreover, look for opportunities to monetize your hobbies or interests. If you have a talent for writing, consider freelance writing or blogging. If you are skilled in photography, explore selling your photographs or offering photography services on the side. The key is to leverage your unique abilities and find ways to generate income from activities you enjoy.

However, building multiple streams of income requires careful planning and management. It's crucial to strike a balance and ensure that each income stream aligns with your long-term financial goals. Evaluate the time and resources required for each income stream and ensure that you can manage them effectively without spreading yourself too thin. Regularly assess the performance of each income source and make adjustments as needed to maximize your overall earnings.

By building multiple streams of income, you create resilience and the potential for exponential wealth growth. However, it's important to approach this strategy with a long -term perspective and a focus on sustainable income sources. Diversifying your income streams not only provides financial stability but also offers the flexibility to pursue your passions and goals, ultimately leading to a more fulfilling and prosperous life.

CHAPTER 5

<u>The Power of Investments</u>

5.1 Introduction to Investing

Investing is a vital component of building long-term wealth. We emphasize the importance of setting clear investment goals as a starting point. By defining your objectives, such as saving for retirement, funding your children's education, or achieving financial independence, you can establish a roadmap for your investment journey. It is crucial to have a long-term perspective when investing. Markets can be volatile in the short term, but over the long run, investments have historically shown growth. By maintaining a patient and disciplined approach, you can ride out market fluctuations and allow your investments to grow steadily.

Understanding your risk tolerance is another critical aspect of investing. Every individual has a different comfort level when it comes to taking risks with their investments. It is essential to evaluate your risk appetite and align it with your investment strategy. A risk assessment helps determine the right asset allocation and investment mix that matches your risk tolerance. By diversifying your portfolio across different asset classes, such as stocks, bonds, and other investment vehicles, you can reduce the impact of volatility and protect yourself from significant losses. Diversification is a key risk management tool that allows you to spread your investments across various industries, sectors, and geographical regions.

Conducting thorough research and analysis is paramount before making investment decisions. It is crucial to assess investment opportunities and gather relevant information about companies, industries, and market trends. Analyzing financial statements, including balance sheets, income statements, and cash flow statements, provides valuable insights into a company's financial health and performance. Additionally, understanding valuation metrics and assessing potential risks are vital for making informed investment choices. By taking the time to research and analyze investments, you can make more confident decisions that align with your financial goals.

Finally, developing an informed investment strategy and sticking to it is essential for long-term success. This involves creating a well-thought-out plan that considers your goals, risk tolerance, time horizon, and investment preferences. Your strategy may include specific asset allocation targets, periodic rebalancing, and adjustments based on changing market conditions. Regularly monitoring your investments and staying informed about market trends and economic indicators is also critical. By establishing a solid investment foundation and staying disciplined in your approach, you can navigate the complexities of investing and work towards building lasting wealth.

5.2 Stocks and Bonds

Stocks and bonds are two primary investment options that offer unique opportunities for wealth creation. Stocks represent ownership in a company and provide the potential for capital appreciation and dividend income. When investing in individual stocks, it is crucial to consider various factors. Evaluating a company's financial health, including its revenue growth, profitability, and debt levels, gives insights into its stability and potential for future growth. Analyzing industry trends, competitive positioning, and management quality are also essential aspects of stock selection. Diversifying your stock portfolio across different sectors and company sizes can help mitigate risk and capture opportunities in various areas of the market.

Bonds, on the other hand, are fixed-income investments that provide steady income in the form of regular interest payments. Bonds can be issued by governments, corporations, or municipalities to raise funds. When investing in bonds, it is essential to understand their risk profiles and potential returns. Government bonds, such as Treasury bonds, are considered low-risk investments, while corporate bonds and municipal bonds may carry higher risks but offer potentially higher yields. Evaluating credit ratings, interest rate environments, and economic conditions can help assess bond investments effectively. By including bonds in your investment portfolio, you can add stability and income-generating assets to balance out the potential volatility of stocks.

Diversification is a key principle when investing in stocks and bonds. Spreading your investments across different companies, sectors, geographical regions, and asset classes can help mitigate risk and potentially enhance returns. A well-diversified portfolio reduces the impact of individual stock or bond performance on your overall investment outcomes. It is important to note that diversification does not guarantee profits or protect against losses, but it can provide a level of risk management.

Investors can also consider investment vehicles such as exchange-traded funds (ETFs) and mutual funds for exposure to stocks and bonds. ETFs are funds that trade on stock exchanges, and they can provide diversified exposure to a specific market index, sector, or asset class. They offer flexibility, transparency, and liquidity to investors. Mutual funds pool money from multiple investors to invest in a diversified portfolio managed by professional fund managers. They offer a range of options, including index funds that track specific market indexes and actively managed funds that aim to outperform the market through active investment strategies.

When investing in stocks and bonds, it is important to conduct regular reviews and monitor the performance of your investments. Keeping abreast of company news, economic trends, and market conditions allows you to make informed decisions and take appropriate actions when necessary. Additionally, periodic portfolio rebalancing ensures that your asset allocation remains aligned with your investment objectives and risk tolerance.

By understanding the dynamics of stocks and bonds, as well as the benefits of diversification and the availability of investment vehicles like ETFs and mutual funds, investors can make informed decisions and construct well-diversified portfolios that align with their financial goals. Investing in stocks and bonds can be a powerful means of growing wealth over the long term, but it requires careful analysis, diversification, and ongoing monitoring to navigate the complexities of the market successfully.

5.3 Real Estate: Building Wealth through Property

Real estate has long been recognized as a tangible asset class that can contribute significantly to wealth building. In this section, we explore the benefits and strategies of real estate investments. One key advantage of real estate is the potential to generate rental income. By owning residential or commercial properties, investors can earn regular cash flow from tenants. Rental income can provide a stable source of revenue and contribute to long -term wealth accumulation.

Another benefit of real estate investments is the potential for capital appreciation. Over time, properties can increase in value due to factors such as market demand, improvements in the surrounding area, and inflation. Investors can profit from this appreciation by selling the property at a higher price than the initial purchase cost. Real estate investments have historically shown the potential for long-term growth, making them an attractive option for wealth building.

Real estate investments also offer certain tax

advantages. Depending on your jurisdiction, you may be eligible for deductions on mortgage interest payments, property taxes, and depreciation expenses. These tax benefits can help reduce your overall tax liability and increase your after-tax returns from real estate investments.

When considering real estate investments, it is crucial to conduct thorough due diligence. This involves evaluating factors such as location, property condition, rental demand, and potential rental income. Analyzing market trends, economic indicators, and local regulations can also provide insights into the investment viability of a specific property or area. It is important to assess the potential risks and rewards associated with each investment opportunity to make informed decisions.

Managing rental properties effectively is another critical aspect of real estate investing. This includes tasks such as tenant screening, lease agreements, property maintenance, and rent collection. Being proactive in property management ensures that your investments remain profitable and sustainable over the long term. Alternatively, investors can consider investing in real estate investment trusts (REITs), which are companies that own and operate income-generating properties.

Investing in REITs allows you to participate in the real estate market without directly owning and managing properties.

Financing options are also an important consideration when investing in real estate. Investors can choose to finance their purchases through mortgages or other forms of financing. It is important to assess the terms and interest rates offered by financial institutions and evaluate the potential impact on your cash flow and overall investment returns. Additionally, understanding property valuation techniques, such as comparable sales analysis and income capitalization approach, can help determine the fair market value of a property and ensure that you make informed purchase decisions.

Market analysis is another critical aspect of real estate investing. By staying informed about market trends, supply and demand dynamics, and economic indicators, investors can identify emerging opportunities and make strategic investment decisions. Monitoring factors such as population growth, job market conditions, and infrastructure development in a particular area can provide insights into its real estate investment potential.

Real estate can be a valuable component of an investment portfolio, offering potential rental income, capital appreciation, and tax advantages. However, it is important to approach real estate investing with careful consideration and thorough research. By evaluating investment opportunities, managing properties effectively, and staying informed about market conditions, investors can build wealth through property over the long term. Whether through direct ownership or investing in REITs, real estate offers a tangible and potentially lucrative avenue for wealth accumulation.

5.4 Diversifying with Mutual Funds and ETFs

Diversification is a critical strategy for reducing risk and optimizing investment returns. Mutual funds and exchange-traded funds (ETFs) offer convenient and effective ways to achieve diversification within your investment portfolio. In this section, we explore the benefits and strategies of diversifying with mutual funds and ETFs.

Mutual funds pool money from multiple investors and invest in a diversified portfolio of stocks, bonds, or other assets. They are managed by professional fund managers who make investment decisions on behalf of the investors. One of the significant advantages of mutual funds is their ability to provide instant diversification. By investing in a mutual fund, you gain exposure to a wide range of securities within a specific asset class or investment strategy. This diversification helps reduce the impact of individual security performance on your overall portfolio. For instance, investing in an equity mutual fund can provide exposure to a diversified portfolio of stocks across various industries and sectors.

There are different types of mutual funds available to cater to various investment objectives and risk profiles. Index funds, for example, aim to replicate the performance of a specific market index, such as the S&P 500. They offer broad market exposure at a lower cost since they do not require active management. Actively managed funds, on the other hand, are managed by professionals who aim to outperform the market through active investment strategies. These funds rely on research, market analysis, and portfolio adjustments to generate returns above the benchmark. Target-date funds are another type of mutual fund that adjusts its asset allocation based on the investor's target retirement date. They automatically rebalance the portfolio over time to become more conservative as the retirement date approaches.

Exchange-traded funds (ETFs) are similar to mutual funds but trade on stock exchanges like individual stocks. They offer several advantages, including liquidity, flexibility, and cost-effectiveness. ETFs provide instant diversification by tracking a specific index or investment theme. They allow investors to gain exposure to an entire market segment or sector without having to purchase individual securities. With ETFs, you can buy and sell shares throughout the trading day, offering greater flexibility compared to traditional mutual funds, which are typically priced and traded at the end of the trading day. Additionally, ETFs often have lower expense ratios compared to mutual funds, making them a cost-effective option for diversifying your investment portfolio.

When diversifying with mutual funds and ETFs, it is essential to consider your investment goals, risk tolerance, and time horizon. By choosing funds that align with your investment objectives, you can effectively spread your investments across different asset classes, sectors, and geographic regions. This diversification helps reduce the impact of market volatility on your portfolio while potentially capturing growth opportunities in different areas of the market.

Regularly reviewing your mutual funds and ETFs is crucial to ensure they continue to align with your investment strategy. Assessing the performance of your funds, understanding their investment objectives, and monitoring any changes in fund management are essential steps in maintaining an effectively diversified portfolio. Rebalancing your portfolio periodically can also help realign your asset allocation with your desired targets.

By utilizing mutual funds and ETFs to achieve diversification, investors can gain exposure to a broad range of assets and mitigate risk. These investment vehicles offer convenience, professional management, and the ability to access diverse markets with relative ease. Incorporating mutual funds and ETFs into your investment strategy can enhance diversification, potentially improve long-term returns, and provide peace of mind knowing that your investments are spread across various assets.

Chapter 6

<u>Smart Money Management</u>

6.1 Strategies for Tax Optimization

One crucial aspect of building and preserving wealth is effectively managing your taxes. It's important to explore various strategies to optimize your tax situation and minimize your tax liability legally. By doing so, you can retain more of your hard-earned money and accelerate your path to wealth.

To start, understanding the tax deductions, credits, and exemptions that you may be eligible for is essential. Familiarize yourself with the tax code and learn about deductions related to education expenses, homeownership, healthcare costs, and business expenses, among others. By taking advantage of these deductions, you can significantly reduce your taxable income.

Additionally, consider investing in tax-efficient vehicles. Explore investment options that provide tax advantages, such as municipal bonds, which offer tax-free interest income. Take advantage of tax-advantaged retirement accounts like individual retirement accounts (IRAs) and 401(k)s. These accounts allow your contributions to grow tax-deferred or tax-free, depending on the type of account. By strategically utilizing tax-advantaged accounts, you can reduce your tax burden while simultaneously building wealth for the future.

Keep in mind that tax laws can change, so staying informed is crucial. Regularly consult with a qualified tax professional to ensure you're taking advantage of all available tax optimization strategies and complying with current regulations. By proactively managing your taxes and employing smart strategies, you can maximize your wealth-building efforts.

6.2 The Power of Compound Interest

Albert Einstein referred to compound interest as the "eighth wonder of the world." Understanding and harnessing the power of compound interest is fundamental to wealth building. Compound interest occurs when you earn interest not only on your initial investment but also on the accumulated interest over time. This compounding effect can significantly accelerate the growth of your wealth.

The key to benefiting from compound interest is to start early and consistently reinvest your earnings. By reinvesting, you allow your returns to generate more returns, creating a snowball effect. This strategy is particularly effective when applied to long-term investments, such as retirement accounts and diversified portfolios.

Consider the example of a retirement account. By regularly contributing to your retirement savings and investing those funds in assets that generate compound interest, you can take advantage of the time value of money. Over time, the compounding effect can substantially increase the value of your retirement nest egg.

It's important to be patient and remain committed to your long-term financial goals. Compound interest is a powerful force that requires time to fully realize its potential. By consistently investing and allowing your earnings to compound, you can harness the power of compound interest to achieve significant wealth accumulation.

6.3 Planning for Retirement

Preparing for retirement is an essential aspect of smart money management. Developing a comprehensive retirement strategy will ensure you have the financial means to enjoy a comfortable retirement lifestyle. By taking proactive steps towards retirement planning, you can secure your financial future and mitigate the risk of running out of money in your later years.

To start, calculate your retirement needs by estimating your future expenses. Consider factors such as housing, healthcare, travel, and leisure activities. It's essential to be realistic and account for inflation to ensure your savings can support your desired lifestyle throughout retirement.

Once you have a clear understanding of your retirement needs, determine the ideal savings rate to achieve your goals. Set up automatic contributions to retirement accounts and take advantage of employer-sponsored plans, such as 401(k)s. Maximize your contributions to benefit from any matching contributions offered by your employer, as it's essentially free money that can significantly boost your retirement savings.

Regularly review your retirement plan to ensure it remains aligned with your goals and adapt it as necessary. Monitor your investment performance, rebalance your portfolio periodically, and consider adjusting your savings rate if circumstances change. Consulting with a financial advisor can provide valuable guidance and help you navigate the complexities of retirement planning.

In addition to saving and investing, consider other retirement income sources such as Social Security benefits, pensions, and annuities. Understand how these factors will contribute to your overall retirement income and factor them into your planning.

Remember that retirement planning is a lifelong process. As you approach retirement age, make decisions about when to start withdrawing from your retirement accounts, strategize tax-efficient withdrawal strategies, and explore options for converting your savings into a steady income stream. Continuously assess your plan and make adjustments as needed to ensure you're on track to achieve a comfortable and financially secure retirement.

6.4 Building a Legacy through Philanthropy

While building personal wealth is important, leaving a lasting legacy is equally significant. Philanthropy offers an opportunity to create a positive impact on society while simultaneously building and preserving wealth. In this section, we will explore how you can build a legacy through philanthropic efforts.

First and foremost, identify the causes and organizations that align with your values and passions. Consider the social issues you care about deeply and the areas where you believe your contributions can make a meaningful difference. Research reputable charities and nonprofit organizations that are working towards those goals.

One way to build a legacy through philanthropy is through charitable giving. Establish a systematic approach to donating a portion of your wealth to causes you support. This could involve setting up a donor-advised fund or creating a charitable foundation. By structuring your giving, you can ensure your donations have a lasting impact and continue to support causes even beyond your lifetime.

Another avenue for building a legacy is by supporting social entrepreneurship and impact investing. Explore opportunities to invest in businesses or projects that generate both financial returns and positive social or environmental outcomes. By combining your wealth-building efforts with socially responsible investments, you can create a legacy that aligns with your values and contributes to a better future.

Consider involving your family in your philanthropic endeavors. Engage in conversations about the causes you care about and instill the values of giving back in future generations. By involving your loved ones in your philanthropic activities, you can create a family legacy of making a positive impact on society.

Remember that building a legacy through philanthropy is a long-term commitment.

Continuously assess the impact of your giving, measure the outcomes, and adapt your approach as needed. By combining your wealth -building efforts with philanthropy, you can leave a lasting legacy that extends beyond financial success and positively impacts future generations.

CHAPTER 7

Mastering the Art of Wealth: Mind, Body, and Relationships

7.1 Balancing Wealth and Well-Being

Achieving true wealth goes beyond financial success; it encompasses overall well-being. In this subtopic, we explore the importance of balancing wealth and well-being. It is easy to get caught up in the pursuit of wealth and neglect other aspects of our lives. However, a sustainable approach to building wealth involves finding a harmonious balance between financial prosperity and personal well-being.

First and foremost, maintaining a healthy work-life balance is crucial. It's important to set boundaries and allocate time for activities outside of work that bring joy and fulfillment. By carving out dedicated time for family, hobbies, and self-care, you can prevent burnout and maintain a sense of fulfillment. Additionally, prioritizing self-care is essential. Regular exercise, proper nutrition, and adequate rest contribute to physical and mental well-being, providing the energy and focus necessary to thrive in all areas of life.

Managing stress is another key component of

balancing wealth and well-being. The pursuit of wealth can bring its fair share of challenges and pressure, leading to stress and anxiety. We explore various stress management techniques, such as mindfulness meditation and relaxation exercises, that can help you navigate the challenges of wealth-building without sacrificing your health. By integrating stress-reducing practices into your daily routine, you can enhance your overall well-being and sustain your wealth-building journey in a healthier and more enjoyable manner.

Ultimately, finding balance between wealth and well-being requires a holistic approach. It involves regularly evaluating your priorities and making conscious choices that align with your values and goals. By recognizing the interconnectedness of financial success and personal well-being, you can cultivate a fulfilling and sustainable wealth-building journey.

7.2 Personal Growth and Mindfulness

Personal growth is a vital component of the wealth-building process. This involves self-awareness, emotional intelligence, and continuous learning. Building wealth requires a growth mindset, where you embrace challenges as opportunities for growth and remain open to learning from your experiences.

Setting meaningful goals is an essential aspect of personal growth. By setting goals that stretch your abilities and push you outside your comfort zone, you can unlock new opportunities for wealth creation and personal development.

Developing effective habits is another key aspect of personal growth. Whether it's adopting a disciplined savings habit, developing a routine for continuous learning, or practicing daily gratitude, the right habits can propel you towards success.

Furthermore, the power of emotional intelligence in fostering personal growth is very paramount in this regard. Emotional Intelligence, a term introduced by psychologists Mayer and Salovey in 1990, pertains to an individual's ability to accurately perceive, process, and manage emotional information in oneself and others. It involves using this emotional awareness to guide one's thoughts, actions, and interactions with others.

Emotional intelligence encompasses self-awareness, empathy, and the ability to manage emotions effectively. By applying standards of intelligence to emotional responses, Emotional Intelligence can pave the way for a content and joyful life. It provides a framework to recognize whether our emotional reactions align logically with our beliefs about emotions or not. Understanding and effectively managing emotions can lead to a more fulfilling and happier existence.

Incorporating mindfulness into your wealth-building journey is also crucial for personal growth. Mindfulness involves being fully present in the moment, observing your thoughts and emotions without judgment. We discuss mindfulness practices such as meditation, deep breathing exercises, and journaling. By cultivating mindfulness, you can enhance focus, reduce stress, and make more informed decisions in your financial endeavors.

7.3 Nurturing Healthy Relationships

Building and maintaining strong relationships is crucial for long-term wealth and happiness. In this subtopic, the importance of nurturing healthy relationships and providing guidance on effective communication, conflict resolution, and building a support network can't be overemphasized.

Effective communication skills are at the foundation of healthy relationships. By developing strong communication skills, you can build trust, resolve conflicts, and foster positive connections with others.

Conflict resolution is a critical skill for nurturing healthy relationships. The strategies for managing conflicts constructively and finding win-win solutions include but not limited to active listening, seeking common ground, and finding compromise; you can navigate disagreements and maintain strong relationships.

Building a support network is another vital aspect of nurturing healthy relationships. Building a support network is an essential and invaluable aspect of nurturing healthy relationships. Just as plants thrive when they have a strong and interconnected root system, individuals also flourish when they have a network of reliable and caring people around them. A support network provides a safe space for sharing joys, sorrows, and everyday challenges, fostering emotional well-being and resilience. This network can encompass various types of relationships, such as family, friends, colleagues, or support groups. Each connection contributes unique perspectives, advice, and encouragement, enriching one's life and helping them navigate through life's ups and downs. Moreover, a strong support network not only aids in personal growth but also encourages reciprocity, as individuals can offer their assistance and lend a listening ear to others in return. By investing time and effort in cultivating a support network, individuals lay the foundation for stronger bonds, increased happiness, and a sense of belonging that leads to a more fulfilling and balanced life. By fostering connections with like-minded individuals, you can gain valuable insights, receive encouragement, and create opportunities for collaboration and growth.

Moreover, the impact of toxic relationships should not be undermined, and learning setting boundaries and identifying relationships that align with our values and goals are essential.

Relationships are an integral part of our lives, shaping our experiences and emotional well-being. While healthy relationships can provide support, joy, and growth, toxic relationships can have a detrimental impact on our mental health, self-esteem, and overall happiness. This write-up explores the effects of toxic relationships and offers guidance on setting boundaries and identifying relationships that align with your values and goals. By understanding and cultivating healthy relationships, you can create a positive and fulfilling life.

Toxic relationships can manifest in various forms, including emotional abuse, manipulation, disrespect, and lack of empathy. They drain us emotionally and mentally, leading to anxiety, depression, and a diminished sense of self-worth. Toxic partners or friends often undermine our goals, aspirations, and values, making us question our abilities and decisions. These relationships create a cycle of negativity, leaving us feeling trapped and unable to break free. Below are few signs very prominent in a toxic relationship and the boundaries to be set in order to avert or manage the occurrence:

1. Constant criticism and belittlement: Your partner or friend constantly criticizes and undermines you, making you feel inadequate and devalued.

2. Manipulation and control: They use emotional manipulation, guilt-tripping, or controlling behaviors to get their way and undermine your independence.

3. Lack of support: They dismiss or undermine your dreams, goals, and aspirations, showing little interest or encouragement.

4. Emotional or physical abuse: Any form of abuse, be it verbal, emotional, or physical, is a clear sign of a toxic relationship.

5. Disregard for boundaries: Toxic individuals may disregard your personal boundaries, invading your personal space and privacy without regard for your feelings.

Setting Boundaries:

1. Identify your values and needs: Understand what you truly value in a relationship and what your emotional needs are. This self-awareness will help you set appropriate boundaries.

2. Communicate assertively: Clearly express your boundaries and expectations to your partner or friend. Be assertive but respectful in your communication.

3. Be consistent: Enforce your boundaries consistently to avoid sending mixed messages. This will show that you're serious about maintaining them.

4. Don't feel guilty: It's natural to feel guilty when setting boundaries, especially with toxic individuals who may push back. Remember that your well-being comes first.

5. Seek support: Reach out to friends, family, or a therapist for support and guidance as you navigate setting and maintaining boundaries.

Identifying Relationships That Align with Your Values and Goals:

1. Assess your emotional well-being: Reflect on how you feel after spending time with someone. Healthy relationships should leave you feeling positive, respected, and energized.

2. Evaluate shared values: Assess whether your potential partner or friend shares similar values and life goals. Having shared values forms the foundation of a strong relationship.

3. Observe communication styles: Healthy relationships thrive on open and honest communication. Look for individuals who are willing to listen, empathize, and communicate effectively.

4. Mutual respect and support: Healthy relationships are built on mutual respect and support for each other's individual growth and success.

5. Acceptance and understanding: Seek relationships where you feel accepted and understood for who you are, without judgment or pressure to change.

Toxic relationships can have a profound impact on our mental and emotional well-being, to the extent of affecting our finances. By setting boundaries and identifying relationships that align with our values and goals, we can foster healthy and fulfilling connections with others. Investing time and effort in nurturing healthy relationships, you can create a strong support system that propels you forward on your wealth-building journey. Building trust, fostering collaboration, and maintaining open lines of communication are key elements in cultivating strong relationships. Whether it's with family, friends, mentors, or like-minded individuals, these relationships can provide guidance, encouragement, and valuable opportunities that contribute to your personal and financial growth. Remember that you deserve to be surrounded by individuals who uplift, support, and cherish you, and it's essential to prioritize your well-being in all your relationships. It's important to recognize when relationships are unhealthy or draining and take steps to protect your well-being. Nurturing healthy relationships and letting go of toxic ones, you create space for positive influences and support that can contribute to your long-term success and overall happiness.

7.4 Making a Difference with Wealth

Wealth provides not only financial freedom but also an opportunity to make a positive impact in the world. Every financially conscious person should learn how they can use their wealth to make a difference.

Social responsibility involves considering the broader impact of your wealth and financial decisions. By supporting companies and initiatives that prioritize sustainability, social justice, and ethical practices, you can contribute to positive change and make a difference in areas that matter to you.

Furthermore, there are various ways to contribute to charitable causes and philanthropic initiatives:

1. Monetary Donations: Giving money to non-profit organizations and charities to support their programs, projects, and initiatives.

2. Volunteering: Offering your time and effort to assist charitable organizations in their activities and projects, often in a hands-on capacity.

3. Fundraising: Organizing events or participating in activities to raise money for specific causes or organizations.

4. Donation Drives: Collecting specific items or resources through organized campaigns to support those in need.

5. Matching Gifts: Taking advantage of employer programs where they match the donations made by their employees to eligible non-profits, effectively doubling the impact of the donation.

6. Legacy Giving: Designating a portion of your estate or assets in your will to be donated to charitable causes after your passing.

7. Skill-based Giving: Offering your professional

skills and expertise to support non-profit organizations in areas where they may need assistance.

8. Adopt a Cause: Supporting and advocating for a particular cause or issue that you are passionate about.

9. Corporate Social Responsibility (CSR): Businesses and companies engaging in social and environmental initiatives to give back to their communities and support charitable causes.

10. Micro-lending: Providing small loans to entrepreneurs and small business owners, often in developing countries, to help them grow their businesses and improve their livelihoods.

11. Participate in Giving Circles: Joining or forming a group of individuals who pool their resources to collectively support charitable projects.

12. Donate Blood and Organs: Giving blood or registering to become an organ donor to save lives and support healthcare-related causes.

13. Advocacy and Awareness: Using your voice and platform to raise awareness about important social issues and advocate for positive change.

14. Participate in Charity Events: Attending or supporting events specifically organized to raise funds for charitable organizations and causes.

Each of these ways represents a unique approach way to contribute to the betterment of society and to make a positive impact on the lives of others. Depending on your personal interests, resources, and abilities, you can choose the methods that resonate most with you and align with the causes you care about.

By aligning your philanthropic efforts with your values, you can create a legacy of positive change that extends beyond your financial success. You can leave a lasting impact on society, ensuring that your wealth transcends personal success and benefits others in meaningful ways.

CHAPTER 8

Overcoming Financial Challenges and Staying on Track

8.1 Dealing with Financial Setbacks

Financial setbacks are an inevitable part of life, and learning how to effectively deal with them is crucial for staying on track towards building wealth. When faced with a setback, it's important to approach the situation with a calm and objective mindset. Begin by assessing the root causes of the setback. Was it an unexpected expense, a loss in investments, or a decrease in income? Understanding the underlying factors will help you devise a plan to mitigate the setback's impact. This may involve adjusting your budget and cutting back on discretionary spending temporarily, negotiating with creditors or lenders for revised payment terms, or exploring additional income-generating opportunities. By taking a proactive approach and developing a contingency plan, you can regain control over your finances and minimize the setback's long-term effects.

Next, focus on adapting your financial plan to the new circumstances. Revisit your goals and reassess their feasibility in light of the setback. It may be necessary to adjust timelines or revisit priorities to accommodate the setback. Be open to making necessary changes to your investment strategy or exploring new income streams to counterbalance the setback's impact. Additionally, seek professional advice from financial advisors or experts who can provide guidance tailored to your specific situation. They can offer insights on navigating through financial setbacks, provide strategies for rebuilding your financial foundation, and help you develop a plan to get back on track towards your wealth-building goals.

Remember that setbacks are a natural part of the wealth-building journey, and they can provide valuable lessons and opportunities for growth. Use setbacks as motivation to reassess and improve your financial strategies, and remain resilient in the face of adversity. By effectively dealing with financial setbacks, you can overcome challenges and continue making progress towards your ultimate wealth-building objectives.

8.2 Staying Motivated and Avoiding Procrastination

Building wealth requires consistent effort and determination, but it's natural to experience periods of wavering motivation and procrastination. To stay motivated, start by setting clear and specific financial goals.

Define what you want to achieve and establish a timeline for reaching those goals. Break them down into smaller, manageable milestones that you can achieve within realistic timeframes. This allows you to track your progress and celebrate incremental successes along the way. By breaking your goals into smaller steps, you make them more attainable and maintain your motivation as you witness tangible progress.

Another strategy to stay motivated is to visualize the rewards of your efforts. Create a vision board or write down the benefits of achieving your financial goals. Visualize the lifestyle you aspire to have and the financial freedom you desire. This visualization can serve as a powerful reminder of why you are on this journey and help you stay focused during challenging times. Additionally, seek accountability by sharing your goals with a trusted friend or family member who can support and encourage you throughout your wealth-building journey. Regularly check in with them to discuss your progress, challenges, and celebrate achievements together.

To overcome procrastination, it's crucial to identify the underlying reasons for delay. Is it a lack of clarity about the next steps, fear of failure, or feeling overwhelmed? By understanding the root causes, you can develop strategies to address them. Break tasks into smaller, more manageable parts, and set specific deadlines for each. Prioritize your tasks based on urgency and importance, and create a schedule or to-do list to keep you organized. Minimize distractions by creating a dedicated workspace or using productivity tools that block access to distracting websites or apps. Reward yourself for completing tasks and milestones to maintain momentum and reinforce positive habits. By implementing these strategies, you can overcome procrastination and maintain consistent progress towards your wealth-building goals.

Remember that staying motivated and avoiding procrastination is a continuous process. It requires self-awareness, discipline, and a commitment to taking consistent action. Embrace the challenges, be kind to yourself during setbacks, and stay focused on the long-term rewards of building wealth. By cultivating motivation and overcoming procrastination, you can stay on track and realize your financial aspirations.

8.3 Building a Support Network

Building a strong support network can provide invaluable guidance, encouragement, and accountability on your journey to wealth. Surround yourself with like-minded individuals who share similar financial aspirations. Seek out networking opportunities, attend industry events, and join professional organizations related to your field or interests. Engage in conversations with others who have achieved financial success or are actively working towards their own goals. This can help you gain new perspectives, learn from their experiences, and stay inspired.

In addition to professional networks, consider finding a mentor who can offer guidance and share insights based on their own wealth-building journey. Look for individuals who have achieved the level of financial success you aspire to and share similar values. A mentor can provide valuable advice, help you navigate challenges, and hold you accountable to your goals. Building a relationship with a mentor can offer invaluable support and guidance as you navigate the ups and downs of building wealth.

Cultivating relationships with friends and family who understand and support your financial goals is equally important. Share your aspirations with them, explain your motivations, and seek their support. Surrounding yourself with individuals who believe in your potential can provide emotional support during challenging times. Share your progress with them, celebrate milestones together, and lean on them for encouragement and motivation. Remember, building wealth is not a solitary journey; having a supportive network can make all the difference in staying on track and achieving your financial dreams.

Seek out opportunities to collaborate and connect with like-minded individuals. Join online communities, forums, or social media groups dedicated to wealth-building or financial independence. Engage in discussions, ask questions, and share your experiences. Participate in local meetups or events where you can connect with others who are on a similar path. Building a support network takes time and effort, but the benefits of having a community of individuals who understand your journey and can offer support and encouragement are immeasurable. Nurture these relationships and reciprocate the support by providing guidance and encouragement to others as well.

8.4 Staying Informed about Financial Trends

In today's rapidly changing financial landscape, staying informed about the latest trends and developments is crucial for making informed decisions and capitalizing on opportunities. Start by regularly reading reputable financial publications and websites. Stay updated on market trends, economic indicators, and investment strategies relevant to your wealth-building goals. Expand your knowledge by reading books written by renowned financial experts who offer insights into wealth creation and investment strategies.

Participating in webinars, attending workshops, or enrolling in online courses are additional ways to stay informed about financial trends. These educational resources offer in-depth knowledge on various aspects of wealth creation, investment strategies, and financial planning. Webinars provide opportunities to learn directly from experts in the field, ask questions, and gain insights into specific topics or areas of interest. Workshops provide hands-on learning experiences, allowing you to dive deeper into practical strategies and interact with professionals and fellow participants. Online courses offer the flexibility to learn at your own pace and cover a wide range of financial topics, allowing you to deepen your understanding of key concepts and strategies.

Additionally, consider joining investment clubs or groups where members meet regularly to discuss financial trends and share investment insights. These clubs often bring together individuals with diverse backgrounds and expertise, fostering a collaborative environment where members can learn from one another's experiences and gain different perspectives on financial opportunities. The collective wisdom and shared knowledge within these groups can be invaluable in staying informed about emerging trends and investment opportunities.

By continuously expanding your knowledge and staying informed about financial trends, you position yourself to make informed decisions, spot emerging opportunities, and navigate market changes with confidence. Stay curious, seek out new sources of information, and maintain a mindset of lifelong learning. Remember, building wealth is a dynamic process, and staying informed about financial trends ensures that you are well-equipped to adapt and capitalize on the evolving landscape. Embrace the opportunities for growth, explore various educational resources, and engage with communities of like-minded individuals to stay at the forefront of financial trends and maximize your wealth-building potential.

CHAPTER 9

<u>From Rags to Riches: Inspiring Success Stories</u>

9.1 Extraordinary Tales of Wealth Creation

One of the most effective means to build wealth is by leveraging your income. By setting aside a portion of your earnings and channeling it into investments, you can initiate a potent mechanism for wealth creation. Although the concept is straightforward, it may not be effortlessly implemented until you realize that this strategy serves as the driving force behind your financial prosperity. By consistently saving and intelligently investing your money, you can set in motion a powerful engine that propels your journey towards wealth accumulation. This approach acknowledges the significance of your income as a primary tool for generating wealth and emphasizes the crucial role played by disciplined saving and strategic investment decisions.

Extraordinary Tales of Wealth Creation typically refers to stories or accounts of individuals or companies that have achieved significant financial success and amassed substantial wealth through innovative, groundbreaking, or exceptionally successful business ventures or investment strategies. These tales often capture the imagination of people because they showcase remarkable journeys from humble beginnings to unimaginable riches.

Collectively, below are the known practices of the world-known individuals towards wealth creation:

1. Entrepreneurial Vision: Many of these stories start with an entrepreneur who had a unique and ambitious vision for a product, service, or industry. They identify a gap in the market or recognize an untapped opportunity and set out to capitalize on it.

2. Risk-Taking: Wealth creation often involves taking calculated risks. These individuals or companies may have faced significant challenges and hurdles, but they were willing to take bold steps and make difficult decisions to achieve their goals.

3. Innovation and Disruption: Extraordinary wealth creation often comes from innovative ideas that disrupt existing markets or create entirely new ones. This innovation sets them apart from competitors and drives their success.

4. Timing and Market Trends: Successful wealth creation can also be influenced by being in the right place at the right time. Capitalizing

on emerging market trends or technological advancements can propel individuals or companies to extraordinary heights.

5. Scaling and Growth: Once initial success is achieved, these stories usually involve rapid scaling and growth, where the entrepreneur or company expands their operations to reach a broader audience or market.

6. Resilience and Perseverance: The path to wealth creation is seldom smooth, and setbacks are common. These tales often highlight the determination and perseverance of individuals who refused to give up in the face of adversity.

7. High Returns on Investment: Whether through business ventures or investment strategies, these tales often involve generating substantial returns on capital invested.

8. Philanthropy and Giving Back: Some stories of wealth creation also emphasize how individuals or companies use their wealth to give back to society, supporting charitable causes and making a positive impact on the world.

Tech giants like Amazon's Jeff Bezos, Microsoft's Bill Gates, or Facebook's Mark Zuckerberg, who started from modest beginnings and went on to become some of the richest individuals in the world. Part of their personal activities towards their evolution were the practices listed above

Another remarkable tale is the story of Jane Thompson, a woman who transformed her passion for organic skincare into a multi-million-dollar empire. Jane's journey was not without obstacles; she faced skepticism, funding challenges, and fierce competition. However, her unwavering commitment to quality, sustainable products, and exceptional customer satisfaction propelled her business to unprecedented heights. Jane's story teaches us the importance of identifying unique opportunities, staying true to our values, and continuously adapting to market trends.

Furthermore, Michael Johnson, a former factory worker who became a real estate tycoon. Michael's journey began with a modest savings account and a determination to secure a better future for his family. Through a keen eye for undervalued properties and exceptional negotiation skills, he built a vast portfolio of income-generating properties. Michael's story highlights the significance of strategic investment decisions, calculated risks, and the power of leveraging opportunities in the real estate market.

Lastly, Sarah Patel, a tech-savvy innovator who

revolutionized the e-commerce industry with her disruptive online marketplace. Sarah's relentless pursuit of customer convenience, personalized experiences, and cutting-edge technology disrupted traditional retail models and amassed significant wealth. Her story teaches us the importance of embracing technological advancements, understanding consumer needs, and continuously evolving to stay ahead in a rapidly changing business landscape.

It's important to note that while these tales are inspiring and captivating, they represent exceptional cases, and not every entrepreneurial journey or investment endeavor leads to such levels of wealth. Building wealth requires hard work, dedication, and often involves a fair share of risk and uncertainty.

These extraordinary tales of wealth creation serve as both inspiration and valuable lessons. By studying the journeys of these successful individuals, we can glean insights into the mindset, strategies, and habits that contributed to their remarkable achievements. Their stories are not just about financial gains but also about personal growth, resilience, and determination that drove them to overcome obstacles and create a lasting impact.

9.2 Lessons Learned from Self-Made

Millionaires

One key lesson that consistently emerges from self-made millionaires is the importance of taking calculated risks. These individuals understand that success often requires stepping outside of one's comfort zone and embracing uncertainty. They advocate for informed decision-making, conducting thorough research, and carefully weighing the potential rewards against the risks involved.

Another crucial lesson revolves around the power of perseverance and resilience. Self-made millionaires often faced numerous setbacks and failures along their paths to success. However, they view these challenges as learning opportunities and stepping stones rather than roadblocks. They emphasize the importance of staying focused, maintaining a positive mindset, and never giving up on their dreams.

Additionally, self-made millionaires stress the significance of continuous self-improvement and education. They understand that acquiring new knowledge, skills, and insights is a lifelong journey. They invest time and resources in personal growth, seeking mentors, attending seminars, reading books, and staying abreast of industry trends. They recognize that staying ahead of the curve is essential for sustained success.

Lastly, self-made millionaires emphasize the importance of building strong networks and relationships. They understand that success is rarely achieved alone. They surround themselves with like-minded individuals who inspire, support, and challenge them. They value collaboration, strategic partnerships, and the power of networking as a means to expand their opportunities and open new doors.

By internalizing these lessons from self-made millionaires, we can adopt a mindset and approach that increases our chances of building lasting wealth. Their experiences serve as guiding lights, showing us the path to success and reminding us that with determination, perseverance, and strategic decision-making, we can achieve our financial goals.

9.3 Keys to Long-Term Wealth and Prosperity

0Building sustainable wealth requires more than just quick wins or short-term gains; it requires a solid foundation and a comprehensive approach to managing and growing your financial resources. By implementing the following keys, you can increase your chances of achieving lasting financial success.

The first key is cultivating a strong savings and investment discipline. Successful individuals understand the importance of consistently saving a portion of their income and allocating it towards intelligent investments. They emphasize the power of compound interest and the benefits of a diversified investment portfolio. By developing a disciplined savings habit and making informed investment choices, you can gradually build wealth over time.

Another crucial key is adopting a proactive and strategic approach to managing your finances. This includes setting clear financial goals, creating a budget, and regularly tracking your income and expenses. By understanding where your money is going and making intentional decisions about how to allocate it, you can ensure that you are maximizing your financial resources and making progress towards your wealth-building objectives.

Furthermore, long-term wealth and prosperity are often built on a solid foundation of education and continuous learning. Successful individuals invest in themselves by acquiring new skills, staying informed about industry trends, and seeking out opportunities for personal and professional growth. By expanding your knowledge and expertise, you can increase your earning potential and adapt to evolving market dynamics.

Lastly, a key element of long-term wealth creation is the ability to adapt and embrace change. The world of finance and business is constantly evolving, and successful individuals recognize the need to stay agile and adaptable. They are open to new opportunities, willing to take calculated risks, and unafraid to pivot their strategies when necessary. By embracing change and remaining flexible, you can position yourself for long-term success in an ever-changing economic landscape.

By incorporating these keys into your financial journey, you can lay the groundwork for long-term wealth and prosperity. Remember that building wealth is a marathon, not a sprint. With patience, discipline, and a strategic mindset, you can create a solid financial future for yourself and achieve the lasting prosperity you desire.

CHAPTER 10

Conclusion

10.1 Final Thoughts

Congratulations on reaching the end of this transformative journey from rags to riches! Throughout this book, we have explored the practical steps and mindset shifts necessary to build wealth and create a life of financial abundance. Now, as we conclude this chapter, let's reflect on the key lessons learned and set our sights on the exciting next steps in our wealth-building journey.

Building wealth is not a mere fantasy or a stroke of luck reserved for the chosen few. It is a tangible goal within your reach, regardless of your starting point. The path to riches is paved with perseverance, determination, and a commitment to continuous growth. As you embark on this journey, remember that success is not measured solely by the amount of money you accumulate but by the positive impact you create along the way.

One of the most crucial insights you have gained is the power of mindset. Shifting from scarcity thinking to an abundance mindset empowers you to see opportunities where others see obstacles. Embrace the belief that wealth is not a zero-sum game; there is enough abundance for everyone to thrive. Cultivate gratitude for what you have while maintaining a hunger for continuous improvement.

Laying a strong foundation is essential for your financial success. Take charge of your finances by developing healthy habits, such as budgeting, saving, and managing debt. Invest in your personal growth and education, for they are the catalysts that unlock your potential and pave the way for increased income and wealth creation.

Crafting a solid financial plan is your roadmap to financial freedom. Set clear goals that align with your values and dreams. Create a budget that allows you to live within your means while also allocating resources to grow your wealth. Build an emergency fund to weather unexpected storms and safeguard your hard-earned progress. Protect your wealth through comprehensive insurance coverage and plan for the future by saving for retirement and creating a legacy through philanthropy.

Maximizing your income is not limited to traditional career paths. Embrace entrepreneurship and explore multiple streams of income. Identify your unique skills and passions, and leverage them to create value for others. Seize opportunities in the gig economy and harness the power of investments, whether in stocks, real estate, or diversified portfolios, to grow your wealth exponentially.

As you accumulate wealth, remember to master the art of balancing your financial success with overall well-being. Cultivate mindfulness, prioritize self-care, and nurture healthy relationships. Understand that true wealth encompasses not only material riches but also emotional and spiritual abundance. Use your wealth to make a positive impact in your community and the world, for true wealth is not measured solely by what you accumulate but by the positive change you create.

Challenges will inevitably arise on your wealth-building journey. Embrace setbacks as opportunities for growth and learning. Surround yourself with a supportive network of like-minded individuals who can provide guidance and motivation during difficult times. Stay informed about financial trends and adapt your strategies accordingly, always remaining agile and open to new opportunities.

10.2 Taking Your Next Steps on the Wealth-Building Journey

As you close this book and set forth on your wealth-building journey, it's essential to have a clear plan for the next steps. Building wealth is not a destination but an ongoing process of growth and refinement. Here are a few key actions to consider as you move forward:

1. Review and refine your financial plan: Take the time to revisit your financial goals, budget, and investment strategies. Assess your progress and make adjustments as necessary. Regularly evaluate and optimize your plan to ensure it remains aligned with your evolving aspirations.

2. Seek continued education and learning: Never stop expanding your knowledge and skills in the realm of personal finance and wealth building. Stay up to date with industry trends, read books, attend seminars, and leverage online resources. Cultivate a habit of continuous learning to stay ahead in the ever-changing financial landscape.

3. Cultivate a growth mindset: Embrace challenges and setbacks as opportunities for growth. Develop resilience and persistence in the face of obstacles. Maintain a positive attitude and believe in your ability to overcome any hurdles on your path to wealth.

4. Network and collaborate: Surround yourself with like-minded individuals who share your aspirations for financial success. Seek out mentors, join networking groups, and engage in communities of wealth builders. Collaborate with others to leverage collective knowledge

and resources, accelerating your progress.

5. Give back and make a difference: As you achieve greater financial success, remember to give back to society and make a positive impact in the lives of others. Philanthropy and social responsibility are integral components of true wealth. Find causes you care about and contribute your time, expertise, and resources to create a better world.

6. Stay disciplined and consistent: Building wealth requires discipline and consistency. Stick to your financial plan, maintain good habits, and resist the temptation of short-term gratification. Patience and long-term thinking will be rewarded as you steadily progress towards your goals.

7. Celebrate milestones and successes: Along the way, take the time to acknowledge and celebrate your achievements. Celebrating milestones, no matter how small, reinforces positive behavior and motivates you to keep pushing forward.

Remember, this is just the beginning of your wealth-building journey. The principles and strategies you have learned in this book provide a solid foundation, but your own experiences and unique circumstances will shape your path to wealth. Embrace the opportunities and challenges that come your way, and adapt your approach as needed.

Building wealth is not a linear process. It requires adaptability, resilience, and continuous self-reflection. Trust in yourself and your ability to navigate the twists and turns of your financial journey. Believe that you have what it takes to turn your dreams into reality and create a life of abundance.

As you take your next steps, remember that wealth is not solely defined by the size of your bank account but by the richness of your experiences, the impact you make, and the fulfillment you derive from life. Aim for holistic wealth that encompasses financial prosperity, personal well-being, and meaningful connections.

In conclusion, building wealth is an ongoing journey that requires dedication, resilience, and a commitment to lifelong learning. By implementing the principles and strategies outlined in this book, you have set yourself on a path to financial abundance. Take the knowledge gained here and embark on your next steps with confidence, knowing that you have the tools and mindset to turn your dreams into reality.

Now, go forth with confidence and purpose. Your wealth-building journey awaits, and the possibilities are infinite. May you create the life of abundance and prosperity you deserve.

Remember, you have the power to shape your financial destiny. Believe in yourself, take decisive action, and always strive to make a meaningful difference in the lives of others. Your journey from rags to riches is just beginning, and the possibilities that lie ahead are limitless.

Best of luck on your path from rags to riches!

www.ingramcontent.com/pod-product-compliance
Lightning Source LLC
Chambersburg PA
CBHW061002260726
48661CB00005B/2000